Liverpool Everyman & Playhouse theatres
present the world premiere of

THE WALRUS HAS A RIGHT TO ADVENTURE

By Billie Collins

First performed on 12 June 2025
at the Everyman theatre, Liverpool

CAST

TASHA DOWD
RIO

REGINALD EDWARDS
OSKAR

PRINCESS KHUMALO
HAZEL

WITH THANKS TO:
LEO CHRYSAKAS, RUBY CLARKE, TOMMI BRYSON, EARL PALMER, ROSA HESMONDHALGH, ANNIE MAY FLETCHER, KATRINE SOLVAAG, WREN WEAVER, TOM ESPINER.

The Walrus Has a Right to Adventure was developed with the support of the National Theatre's Generate programme.

COMPANY

WRITER
BILLIE COLLINS

DIRECTOR
NATHAN CROSSAN-SMITH

SET & COSTUME DESIGNER
CHLOE WYN

LIGHTING DESIGNER
RAJIV PATTANI

COMPOSER & SOUND DESIGNER
OLIVER VIBRANS

VOICE COACH
RACHEL NICHOLSON

YEP TRAINEE ASSISTANT DIRECTOR
ABBIE CASKIE

DRAMATURG
TOMMO FOWLER

PRODUCER
MICHELLE CAILLEUX

PRODUCTION MANAGER
DIEGO GUTIÉRREZ CÓRDOBA

COMPANY MANAGER
SARAH LEWIS

STAGE MANAGER
KAILA SHARPLES

DEPUTY STAGE MANAGER
ROXANNE VELLA

ASSISTANT STAGE MANAGER
PHIL CLACK

BOOK COVER
BETH LEWIS-CLAREY

ASSISTANT PRODUCER
ZOE WALKER

LX PROGRAMMER
JACK WOOD

LX SUPPORT
ANDY WEBSTER

LX OPERATOR
JENNIFER CHISLETT

SENIOR SOUND TECHNICIAN
IAN DAVIES

SOUND 1
IAN DAVIES, JACK WOOD

SENIOR STAGE TECHNICIAN
MIKE CANTLEY

STAGE FIT-UP CREW
DAVE MCGOVERN, KEITH HOLT, OLLY MORRIS

COSTUME SUPERVISOR
CATE MACKIE

SET CONSTRUCTION
LIVERPOOL SCENIC, OLLY MORRIS

SCENIC ART
ABBIE JONES

AUDIO DESCRIBED PERFORMANCE
MICHAEL HURST FOR MINDS EYE

CAPTIONED PERFORMANCE
KAY GEORGE

COVER PHOTOGRAPH
KERRY SPICER

TASHA DOWD | RIO

Tasha Dowd graduated from Leeds Conservatoire with a BA (Hons) in Actor Musicianship and has been working in and around their home city ever since. Having been part of the development for The Walrus Has a Right to Adventure early on, they can't wait to take to the stage as Rio Taylor and sink their teeth into this exciting show!

Credits for the Everyman & Playhouse include: as writer *Tell Me How It Ends* (Liverpool Everyman).

Theatre credits include: *The Storm and The Minotaur* and *The Coup Coup Club* (Slung Low Warehouse); *Stocking Fillers* (Liverpool Royal Court); *Joy Unspeakable* (Ordinary Glory); *Cinderella* (Chester Storyhouse); *Vernons Girls* (Liverpool Royal Court) and *Macbeth* (Leeds Playhouse).

Tv credits include: *Tin Star* (Season 3, Sky Atlantic).

REGINALD EDWARDS | OSKAR

Theatre credits includes: *Great Expectations* (Manchester Royal Exchange); *A Christmas Carol*, *Hamlet* and *Frankenstein* (TNT/ADG Europe); *Brighton Beach Memoirs* (Frinton Summer Theatre); *The Comeback Special* and *The Collector* (Hope Street Theatre); *The Tempest* (Iris Theatre, St.Paul's Church); *A Peril of the Sea* (Lakeside Theatre); *You're Human Like The Rest Of Them* and *Sommer 14* (Finborough Theatre); *King Lear* (Royal & Derngate / UK tour); *Pride and Prejudice* and *A Midsummer Night's Dream* (Cunard) and *Lotty's War* (UK Tour).

Tv credits include: *Anne* (World Productions for ITV) and *Holby City* (BBC).

PRINCESS KHUMALO | HAZEL

Princess Khumalo is a Zimbabwean-British actor who grew up in the north of Yorkshire. She graduated LIPA in 2021.

Liverpool Everyman & Playhouse credits include: *The Streets Where We Live* (Falling Doors, Liverpool Everyman & Playhouse).

Theatre credits include: *Never Let Me Go* (Rose Theatre Kingston, Bristol Old Vic); *The Independent Socialist Republic of The Upper End of The Lower Breck Road* (Liverpool's Royal Court, The Other Room); *We Need New Names* (Brixton House, Fifth Word, New Perspectives); *The Ultimate Pickle* and *Half Empty Glasses* (Paines Plough); *A Sudden Violent Burst of Rain* (Paines Plough, The Gate Theatre); *Sleepover* (All Things Considered Theatre Company) and *Thats What She Said* (Out The Attic).

Screen credits include: *Holier Than Thou* – 'Best comedy program' Royal Television Society nominee (DAVE); *Doctors* (BBC) and *So Awkward* (CBBC).

BILLIE COLLINS | WRITER

Billie Collins is a writer from the Wirral, currently based in Manchester. Billie also works as a dramaturg and facilitator and is a BBC Writersroom Northern Voices graduate. The lead the Young Writers programme at the Royal Exchange Theatre and are published by Nick Hern Books.

Their recent work includes: *Peak Stuff* (Thickskin Theatre, UK tour); *Too Much World at Once* (Box of Tricks Theatre, UK tour); *Saga* (BBC radio 4) and episodes of *Malory Tower* series 5 and 6 (King Bert productions for CBBC).

NATHAN CROSSAN-SMITH | DIRECTOR

Nathan is a director and practitioner from Manchester. He is Co-Director for immersive company Hydrocracker and a Trustee for disability-led company Graeae. He is Associate Lecturer in directing at the University of Manchester, a National Theatre Connections mentor director and National Youth Theatre Associate Artist. He is a Deutsche Bank Award Winner and Runner up for both the Sir Peter Hall RTST Directors Award and JMK Award and a Finalist for the Genesis Directors Award. He is currently training on Royal Ballet & Opera's inaugural OPERA LAB: MAKING THE FUTURE OF OPERA programme, part of the Jette Parker Artist Programme for 2024/25. He trained at LAMDA and the National Theatre's Directors Course.

Everyman & Playhouse Credits include: *A Monster Calls* (YEP, Liverpool Everyman).

Director credits include: *The Trails* (Storyhouse); *WHO CARES 2032* (Hydrocracker, Royal and Derngate Northampton); *Romeo and Juliet* (Orange Tree); *Richard II* and *Much Ado About Nothing* (LAMDA); *Bitch Boxer* and *Love and Information* (Performers College, Manchester); *Tender Crush* (Donmar Warehouse, Take the Stage); *The Voyage Out (After Virginia Woolf)* (Northern School of Contemporary Dance Research Commission); *Hurricane Protest Songs* (Graeae); *Doorstep Theatre* (November Club); *140bpm* (National Theatre Learning); *Before it Rains* (National Youth Theatre); *Fire in the Youth, My Story, Dreamscape* (National Theatre Wales, as lyricism associate) and *20 Stories of Home* (20 Stories High).

Associate Director credits include: *Operation Black Antler* (Dir. Matt Adams, Blast Theory & Hydrocracker, Southbank Centre) and *Strangers on a Train Set* (Dir. Laurence Till, Lipservice National Tour).

Film & audio credits include: *MISH + GRAHAM* by Thea Gajic and Rebecca Saffir and *Before the Flame Goes Out* by Raymond Antrobus (Hydrocracker); *Half Blue* by Ava Wong Davies (Audible); *Bloodyminded* (as Second AD, Blast Theory, 14-18 NOW) and *A Place Free Of Judgement* (as Floor Manager, Blast Theory).

CHLOE WYN | SET & COSTUME DESIGNER

Chloe Wyn is a set and costume designer based in the North West. Originally from North Wales, Chloe studied Theatre and Performance Design at LIPA, graduating with first-class honours in 2020.

or *The Walrus Has a Right to Adventure*, I've had the joy of designing both the set and costumes. The play spans wildly different locations—from the icy Norwegian fjords to the peaks of Colorado and a Tesco in Halewood—and I wanted the design to reflect that sense of movement, contrast, and wonder. I was especially excited to explore textures in the design, using materials that evoke nature, human, and the surreal, often within the same scene. It was a fantastic opportunity to play with visual contrasts that mirror the story's emotional journey.'

Liverpool Everyman and Playhouse credits include: *Animal Farm* (Liverpool Everyman).

Previous work includes: *These Majestic Creatures* (The Stephen Joseph Theatre, Scarborough); *A Christmas Carol* (Manchester School of Theatre) and *Remix* (Box of Tricks)

RAJIV PATTANI | LIGHTING DESIGNER

Rajiv trained at LAMDA in 2014 and graduated with qualifications in Stage Management and Technical Theatre.

Theatre credits include: *In Search Of Goldoni* (Beyond Face/Bristol Old Vic/Plymouth Drum/Tour); *Heisenberg* (Arcola Studio 2); *Elmer Adventure* (Tall Stories Tour); *The Society For New Cuisine* (Fun Guy Productions); *Alice in Wonderland* (Poltergeist Theatre Co/Brixton House); *Elmer Adventure* (The Lowry/Southbank Centre); *Nowhere* (Fuel Theatre); *Peanut Butter & Blueberries* (Kiln Theatre); *Some Demon* (Papatango, Arcola Theatre); *Test Match, The Maladies, Yellowman, Statements After an Arrest Under the Immortality Act* and *OUTSIDE* (Orange Tree); *10 Nights* (Omnibus/Tour); *Bonfire* (Derby Theatre/Sheffield Theatre/Nonsuch); *High Times and Dirty Monsters* (20 Stories High/Graeae/Liverpool Everyman/LEEDS 2023/Tour); *Strategic Love Play* (Soho Theatre/Paines Plough Roundabout/Tour); *£1 Thursdays* (Finborough Theatre); *The Garden of Words* (Park200); *Sorry, You're Not a Winner* (Paines Plough Tour); *Kabul Goes Pop: Music Television Afghanistan* (Brixton House); *SMOKE* (Southwark Playhouse/3Heart Canvas); *Yellowfin* (Southwark Playhouse); *Wolfie* (Theatre 503); *Mog the Forgetful Cat* and *Winners* (Wardrobe Ensemble); *Final Farewell* and *Dawaat* (Tara Theatre); *Dismantle This Room* (Royal Court Downstairs) and *Babylon Beyond Boarders, Leave Taking* and *Ramona Tells Jim* (Bush Theatre).

OLIVER VIBRANS | COMPOSER & SOUND DESIGNER

Oliver Vibrans is an Ivor Novello award-winning, and RPS award-nominated Composer and Producer based in the UK. Oliver has composed music for the concert hall, theatre, film, art installations and radio.

Recent commissions include: *The Virtuous Circle* (the BBC Proms); *Monomyth* (the Halle); music for two episodes of *Charles Hazelwood's landmark documentary Reinventing the Orchestra* (Sky Arts); *Treading Water* (the BBC Philharmonic and BBC Radio 3); *More Up* (The Halle, BBC Philharmonic and The Able Orchestra, winner of an Ivor Novello award, nominated for a Royal Philharmonic Society award 2020); *Trip the Light Fantastic* (Paraorchestra); *Suspended Dance* (BBC Radio 3); The Composers Postcard Project, *From the Crowd*, a commemoration of Peterloo - part of the unveiling of the memorial by Jeremy Deller; BBC Radio 3's Music And Meditation podcast (BBC Concert Orchestra).

Theatre credits include: *Burnt At The Stake* (Shakespeare's Globe); *Oliver Twist* (Leeds Playhouse and Ramps on the Moon); *Rutherford & Sons* (Sheffield Theatres); *The Solid Life Of Sugar Water* and *Duet* (One for The Orange Tree Theatre); *Romeo And Juliet* (Shakespeare North Playhouse); *The Secret Garden* (Theatre Royal Bury St Edmunds); *This Is Not For You,* an outdoor contemporary opera for 14-18 Now (Graeae GDIF); *A Leap In The Dark* and *The Pitmen Painters* (The New Vic); *The Tempest* (Royal Exchange); *Out of the Dark* (Rose Theatre Kingston) and *Edward II* (Cambridge Arts Theatre).

ABBIE CASKIE | YEP TRAINEE ASSISTANT DIRECTOR

Abbie Caskie is a queer theatre maker from Liverpool, with a passion for telling stories surrounding female and / or queer narratives. Abbie has 5+ years of experience within the industry as a dresser, crew member and acting tutor. She is an LJMU graduate, where she co-founded a small theatre company Bunny Boiler Productions. *The Walrus Has A Right To Adventure* is Abbie's professional debut as a Trainee Assistant Director.

Abbie is currently working alongside Grin Theatre as a writer / director in their upcoming showcase *Queertet,* developing a modern adaptation of Pride and Prejudice called *They're Just Roommates.*

LIVERPOOL EVERYMAN & PLAYHOUSE

Liverpool's theatres, Sparking Creativity and Nurturing Talent

Rooted in Liverpool's spirit, the Everyman & Playhouse are a creative powerhouse with national and international impact, driven by a passion for theatre, the city, and the belief that theatre can entertain, inspire and fuel positive social change.

With two distinctive venues, each rich in history, they offer unforgettable experiences that captivate the imagination and ignite curiosity. Producing local stories with national impact, they champion emerging talent, innovative storytelling and breathe new life into the classics. Liverpool Everyman & Playhouse want to be the most exciting places to experience and create theatre.

A registered charity (1081229), the theatres acknowledge the continued support of Arts Council England and Liverpool City Council, and their audiences, donors, patrons and partners.

For audiences, artists, and communities alike, Liverpool Everyman & Playhouse are places of wonder, magic, and extraordinary moments waiting for you to enjoy.

everymanplayhouse.com

 @livEveryPlay  /everymanplayhouse

FOR THE EVERYMAN & PLAYHOUSE

Executive Team
Mark Da Vanzo Chief Executive
Nathan Powell Creative Director
Ros Thomas Finance Director

Artistic Team
Michelle Cailleux Producer
Tommo Fowler New Works Associate
Erenie Mavrommatis Artistic Administrator
Ashlie Nelson Head of Producing & Programming
Zoe Walker Assistant Producer

Production Team
Michael Cantley Senior Technician (Stage)
Jennifer Chislett Technician (Multi-skilled)
Ian Davies Senior Technician (Sound & AV)
Dan Franklin Head of Production
Diego Gutiérrez Córdoba Assistant Production Manager
Jack Higham Technician (Multi-skilled)
Beth Lewis-Clarey Production Coordinator
Sarah Lewis Company Manager
Cate Mackie Head of Costume
Robert Newman Senior Technician (Sound & AV)
Jennifer Tallon-Cahill Technical Manager
Andy Webster Senior Technician (Lighting)
Jack Wood Technician (Multi-skilled)

Young People & Community
Moira Callaghan Community & Education Manager
Ruth Hall Young People's Advocate
Hayley Lindley-Thornhill Head of Young People & Community
Kieran Sing Young People & Community Technical Manager
Helen Webster Young People & Community Producer

Operations & Administration
Vicki Adlard Head of Administration
Helen Griffiths Operations Manager
Sarah Kelly Executive Assistant
Lynsey Wilson HR Officer

Estates
Antony Delamere Facilities Technician
Jonathan Doherty Cleaning & Facilities Team
Luis Miguel Fernandez Facilities Assistant
Chloë Fisher Cleaning Team
Ed Freeman IT Officer
Ged Manson Cleaning Team
Dominic Phillips Head of Estates
Ian Redden Cleaning Team
Wesley Warren Cleaning Team
Chantal Warren Cleaning Team
Jeffrey Watts Cleaning Team

Audience Experience
Leah Abbott Audience Experience Coordinator (Box Office & Stage Door)
Abbie Bates Audience Experience Manager (Resources)
Brendan Douglas Head of Audience Experience
James Eadan Duty Manager (Hospitality & Events)
George Fragakis Audience Experience Duty Manager (Box Office & Stage Door)
Rory Gillan Duty Manager
Jules Goddard Audience Experience Duty Manager (Box Office & Stage Door)
Melissa James Duty Manager (Front of House)
Andrew King Box Office & Stage Door Manager
Jason Kelly Audience Experience Assistant (Box Office & Stage Door)
Mike Lancaster Audience Experience Manager (Bars & Events)
Kathy Lawrence Audience Experience Assistant (Box Office & Stage Door)
Gary Lun Audience Experience Assistant (Box Office & Stage Door)
Hermionë Marshall Audience Experience Assistant (Box Office & Stage Door)
Jack Molloy Duty Manager
Julia Molteberg Duty Manager (Hospitality & Events)
Ian Nenna Audience Experience Assistant (Box Office & Stage Door)
Gillian Parry Audience Experience Assistant (Box Office & Stage Door)
Harry Sargent Audience Experience Assistant (Box Office & Stage Door)
Raquel Teixeira Duty Manager
Leah Wallace Audience Experience Duty Manager (Box Office & Stage Door)
Hywell Wilkie Duty Manager (Hospitality & Events)

Commercial
Elise Donnelly Catering Manager
Rachel Elliott-Newton Venue & Events Planner Manager
Ruth O'Neill Head of Commercial Development

Finance
Stephen Dickson Finance Manager
Rose Hart Finance Assistant
Nicola Jackson Finance Officer

Marketing & Fundraising
Eleanor Bartley Graphic Design Officer
Olivia Carroll Marketing Officer
Rosalind Gordon Fundraising Manager
Ellie Luke Marketing Assistant
Gemma Murrell Marketing Manager
Sarah Ogle Marketing & Communications Director
Chun-Mei Wang Communications Officer

Thanks to all our Audience Experience Team

Trustees for the Liverpool and Merseyside Theatres Trust Limited

Andrea Nixon (Chair), Saphena Aziz, James Bierman, Natasha Bucknor, Laura Collier, Paul Evans, Portia Fahey (LCC Representative), Jill Jones, Paul Kallee-Grover MBE, Julie Ledder, Paul Maddock, Camilla Mankabady, Caroline Sanger-Davies, Tony Smith.

THANK YOU

Liverpool Everyman & Playhouse are a registered charity (1081229) and gratefully acknowledge the support of our funders, donors, patrons, partners and audiences.

For their ongoing financial support, we would like to thank

 Supported using public funding by **ARTS COUNCIL ENGLAND** **Culture Liverpool**  **Liverpool City Council**

The Austin and Hope Pilkington Trust, Backstage Trust, The Foyle Foundation, Garfield Weston Foundation, Idlewild Trust, The Ken Dodd Foundation

Our HE Partner
Edge Hill University

Our Business members & sponsors
Benson Signs, Bruntwood, Duncan Sheard Glass, Hope Street Hotel, Knowsley Chamber of Commerce, Liverpool Growth Platform, Liverpool and Sefton Chamber of Commerce, Professional Liverpool, Rathbone Investment Management, Wirral Chamber of Commerce, Wrightsure Insurance Group

Our Alumni supporters
Jim Broadbent, Matthew Kelly, Sir Ian McKellen, David Morrissey, Bill Nighy, Eddie Redmayne, Willy Russell, Julie Walters

Our Patrons
Steve and Lorraine Groves, Alan Sprince, Lara and Richie Pearn, John and Mary Belchem, Robin Bloxsidge and Nick Riddle, John Birkenhead, Andrea Nixon and Dan Stinson Paul Herbert, Cath and Phil Kightley

Those who have left a Legacy or gave an In Memory gift
Dorothy Smellie, Anni Parker & Brian Barry, lovers and supporters of theatre, Malcolm & Roger Frood in memory of Graham & Joan Frood, Michael Key, Fanchon Frolich, The Dunham Family in loving memory of Matthew Dunham, Board Member and friend

Those who give monthly or annually for their continued support and to everyone who supported the new Everyman Ev4Ev campaign, our Young Everyman and Playhouse appeal in 2022/23, and our Everyone Starts Somewhere campaign in 2024/25.

THE WALRUS HAS A RIGHT TO ADVENTURE

Billie Collins

'Sometimes a wild god comes to the table
[...] And brings the dead to life.'

Tom Hirons

Characters

OSKAR LYNGSTAD, *he/him, forty-four, a tour guide from Oslo, Norway*

HAZEL CURTIS, *she/her, twenty-eight, a recruitment consultant in Colorado Springs, USA*

RIO TAYLOR, *she/her, later they/them, twenty, a shelf-stacker from Liverpool, England*

Notes

Dialogue in **bold** is in real time.

The play is written for a cast of three. Characters other than Oskar, Hazel and Rio should be shared between the actors not currently narrating. For example, the actor playing Oskar could play Aiden in Hazel's story, the actor playing Rio could play Karolin in Oskar's – and so on.

There are wild animals in this play. How they appear onstage is up to you, but I would steer away from the literal. Use your imagination.

This text went to press before the end of rehearsals and so may differ slightly from the play as performed.

PART ONE: THE ENCOUNTER

A stage. An everywhere-and-nowhere sort of place.

OSKAR, RIO *and* HAZEL *are here.*

They take stock of the room, the audience, each other…

…Yep, that's a room alright! We've seen rooms before. Not to brag, but we're pretty au fait with 'rooms'.

And this one, let's face it, is fairly standard.

They do whatever they need to do to get ready. Maybe there are microphones that need checking. Maybe something is in the wrong place. We're tuning up an orchestra here!

Before they get too comfy, somebody does something – or something happens – which tells us it's time to begin.

Ready? Let's take a run-up…

OSKAR. Oskar.

HAZEL. Hazel.

RIO. Rio.

OSKAR. Oslo.

RIO. Liverpool.

HAZEL. Colorado Springs.

OSKAR. When the story starts, I'm heading to work.

HAZEL. I'm eating breakfast.

RIO. I'm taking a break.

OSKAR. And then –

RIO. And then –

HAZEL. And then he says –

AIDEN. **I'll come with you.**

HAZEL. He's started doing that lately. Inviting himself along to things.

Oh no, Aiden, you don't have to.

AIDEN. **But I want to. And I think it's important we share our hobbies.**

HAZEL. I don't want him to come for two reasons.

The first is he's just not very fast.

And I can't be faster than him, because then he gets all – y'know –

AIDEN. **Joel and Christine play volleyball. Pablo and Nick have started horticulture.**

HAZEL. The second reason is that I go running to be alone with my thoughts.

AIDEN. **I mean it, Hazel. This could be our thing.**

HAZEL. And this run – *this run* in particular, I've been really looking forward to. Four miles of the Red Rock Canyon trail, spectacular views of Pikes Peak. They call it the Gateway to Heaven.

He grabs a protein bar and puts on his sneakers.

They're brand new. Bright yellow. Like, NASCAR yellow.

AIDEN. **I'm coming with you.**

HAZEL. He says again. This time, telling not asking.

Then he takes my keys, and he leads the way.

OSKAR. I arrive at the fjord as I always do. Seven-thirty a.m.

My first tour starts at eight. I run my lines as I head for the water.

This boat once belonged to my father, who was a fisherman here in Oslo, a profession that dates back generations in my family.

They'll eat that up – tradition, inheritance. If I say 'Viking' they will ejaculate into their trousers.

I keep Pia on a short leash as we pass the Fiskehall. She's a good dog, but she can't resist mackerel.

My boat is moored at Vippetangen – less footfall than Aker Brygge or Bjørvika – but it has a 'best-kept secret' kind of feeling that tourists appreciate.

Usually, this area is open to the public. Today it is fenced off…

…And there are fishermen, tourists, a policeman shouting –

POLICE. **Vent! Stand back!**

Pia barks.

OSKAR. **Down, girl. Shh!**

I push to the front.

POLICE. **I said stand back. Don't get too close!**

OSKAR. And there it is. My boat.

Right where I left it.

But not *how* I left it.

A subtle shift. Maybe the world has tilted. Maybe everything is sinking.

The bow noses the air as the stern sinks into the water. It looks like a cartoon, frozen mid-capsize, and resting on the deck…

We get the sense there is a walrus.

A hulking mound of grey-brown flesh.

Pia barks. The beast barks back. The policeman stands in my way.

POLICE. **I'm afraid there's no entry to the pier today.**

OSKAR. **But that's my boat.**

POLICE. **That's your boat?**

OSKAR. **Yes. Well. My pappa's.**

Pause.

POLICE. **Sir... I think it belongs to the walrus now.**

RIO. There's a wasp in the break room. Can't see it yet, but I can hear it.

Suddenly, the room feels a whole lot smaller.

Which is funny, cos the Tesco break room probably feels quite big to the wasp.

I try to ignore it, scroll through my phone.

Text from Lacey asking me to get breakfast after my shift. Yellow-sticker cinnamon swirls.

I check Co–Star. The horoscope app? Lacey made me get it. I don't believe in that stuff, but – well, I'm a Libra with a Pisces moon, which checks out to be honest, so…

Libra. Today you might feel a little glum. Expect a visit from an unusual stranger.

MARTIN. **Is something buzzing in here?**

RIO. Martin. My manager.

There's a wasp. I opened the window.

Martin makes the room feel even smaller.

MARTIN. **I expect you're scared, aren't you? Women are scared of wasps.**

Pause.

You should get back to work.

RIO. **I've still got ten minutes.**

MARTIN. **Scared of wasps, scared of work. Off you pop, Riona. I'll take care of this.**

RIO. He grabs the *Echo* from the coffee table and rolls it into a blunt instrument.

The wasp keeps hitting the window.

Thwack... Thwack... Thwack...

OSKAR. An hour later, the walrus has not moved.

I take Pia up to the ticket office to cancel today's tours.

INGRID. **All of them?**

OSKAR. Ingrid from the ticket office smiles when she sees me.

Her smile makes me smile, even as I am saying –

They can't exactly move him.

INGRID. **Beklager, Oskar. Is there anything I can do?**

OSKAR. **We just have to wait.**

INGRID. **Are you sure?**

OSKAR. **Actually... Could you take Pia for a few hours? If I'm not working, I should see my pappa.**

INGRID. **Of course. How is he doing?**

OSKAR. **Oh, you know... The same.**

Ingrid is, I think, the most beautiful woman in the world.

Pause.

OSKAR *should probably leave now, but he doesn't.*

INGRID. **Is that everything?**

OSKAR. **You changed your hair.**

INGRID. **Søren! I've been trying to hide it. Totally not what I asked for.**

OSKAR. I am a walrus in comparison.

I think it looks good.

INGRID. **That's kind, Oskar.**

Pause.

Shall I take Pia?

OSKAR. **Ja, beklager. Takk.**

He hands over the lead.

INGRID. **A walrus, huh?**

OSKAR. **I know. Crazy.**

INGRID. **I think it's good luck.**

OSKAR. **How can a walrus on my boat be good luck?**

INGRID. **Look at it this way. The day can't get any worse.**

RIO. I leave Martin swatting the wasp and brace myself for the shop floor.

The night shift is when we get our most… interesting customers.

Martin calls them 'creatures'.

MARTIN. **All these creatures, skulking round the aisles.**

RIO. There's the man who sings Barry White and only ever buys condoms.

The woman who steals yogurt and calls you a vegan Nazi if you try stop her.

Quiet Rob, who lost his mum last year…

I take a deep breath, open the door, blink in the lights and…

Slip. Arse over tit.

The floor is sticky with blood – or – no, actually…

I follow the trail round to World Foods and find a busted tin of Heinz Tomato.

VINNIE. **Psst. Rio. Rio!**

RIO. Vinnie's on security. He's crouched behind a display of gourmet cat food.

Vin? What are you doing?

VINNIE. **Come here.**

RIO. **Why?**

A shift. Maybe the world feels too bright, too loud, too much. We get the sense there's a stag.

It is *huge*. Pure white, white as snow, with two massive antlers crowning its head; tall and strong and hard and sharp.

It comes flying round the aisle, hooves clattering on the lino, and it keeps *burping* – big throaty belches echoing off the walls.

Fuck. There's a stag in the Halewood Tesco.

OSKAR. I open the door to find him sat up in bed, unshaven and miserable.

Hallo, Pappa.

He used to be a jotun. A giant. Now he cannot shit without help.

PAPPA. **How is the boat?**

OSKAR. These days he forgets things – names, dates, whether he took his medication. But he *never* forgets the boat.

How are you?

PAPPA. **The boat, Oskar, how is it?**

OSKAR. **The boat is fine, Pappa.**

He does not need to know.

PAPPA. **It should've stayed a fishing boat. We are a fishing family.**

OSKAR. Every time, the same conversation. I could write his lines.

PAPPA. **My only son. A tour guide.**

OSKAR. He says, 'tour guide' as you might say 'pervert' or 'Satanist'.

PAPPA. **Pandering to Americans. Your farfar would be so ashamed.**

OSKAR. **I'm sorry, Pappa. I don't mean to let you down.**

HAZEL. Aiden is doing better than expected.

> Sure, I'm slowing down for him, but only a little, and he hasn't noticed.

AIDEN. **See? What did I tell you?**

HAZEL. Maybe he's right? Maybe I was being uptight. I can be uptight sometimes.

AIDEN. **It's pretty beautiful out here, huh?**

HAZEL. We're surrounded by rock formations. Blood-red sandstone, it's like… running on Mars.

AIDEN. **Hey, just think… when we have kids, we can take them hiking out here.**

HAZEL. **What?**

AIDEN. **When we have kids. I want to be one of those outdoorsy kinda families.**

HAZEL. **Mm.**

AIDEN. **Hazel… I'd like to talk about trying again.**

HAZEL. The trail stretches out ahead of us – a straight line through the trees.

AIDEN. **I know last time wasn't… And you said you needed space, and I've given you space –** *and* **time – I've waited, and I think we're ready to try again. Don't you?**

HAZEL. **Can we maybe talk about this later?**

AIDEN. **Come on, Hazelnuts. You'd be a great mom.**

HAZEL. I keep running.

AIDEN. **Hazel! Slow down!**

HAZEL. I run faster.

RIO. There's gourmet cat food *everywhere*.

> Martin bursts out the breakroom like –

PART ONE: THE ENCOUNTER   13

MARTIN. **I got the wasp!**

RIO. But then sees we've got bigger problems.

> The stag thrashes about, antlers tearing the ceiling.

> Someone must've heard the commotion cos the bizzies are here already. They crash in like something from a Tom Hardy film.

POLICE. **Get in the staffroom, NOW.**

RIO. But my feet won't move.

> Cos one of them has a gun. A *proper* gun.

> And he's pointing it right at the stag.

HAZEL. **I'm fine, Aiden, honestly.**

AIDEN. **Just slow down so we can talk.**

HAZEL. **We're on a run, let's just enjoy the run!**

AIDEN. **Hazel. Stop.**

HAZEL. At this point we're pretty high up. We're not even on the trail any more, we're…

Where are we?

AIDEN. **Don't change the subject –**

HAZEL. **It looks like someone's been camping out here.**

AIDEN. **So?**

HAZEL. **It's not allowed. They left their cooler.**

AIDEN. **Hazel, please. I want to talk. Like real adults.**

HAZEL. **What do you want to talk about?**

AIDEN. **I want to talk about us. I want to talk about –**

HAZEL. **Kids? You can't just spring that on me –**

AIDEN. **But I *have* to – because every time I try to have the conversation –**

HAZEL. **Maybe I'm not ready to talk.**

AIDEN. **I know it's scary, but you're not – we're not – getting any younger. And you said you wanted this. We want this. We want a family, don't we?**

HAZEL. Aiden's NASCAR sneakers are glowing in the sun.

AIDEN. **We want to be happy; we want to secure our future.**

HAZEL. **I know, but – what about –**

AIDEN. **That was a – a… That won't happen again.**

HAZEL. **How do you know?**

AIDEN. **I love you, Hazel.**

HAZEL. My stomach drops.

AIDEN. **I want to spend the rest of my life with you.**

HAZEL. There's sweat on my palms, the back of my neck –

AIDEN. **You are everything to me and –**

HAZEL. **Aiden. Stop.**

AIDEN. **No, listen. You are my everything and –**

HAZEL. **Aiden. Don't. Move.**

A shift. Maybe the world feels dense, heavy, and slow. We get the sense there is a bear.

It's a bear.

AIDEN. **What?**

HAZEL. **A bear. Behind you.**

Her lips peel back. She paws the ground.

AIDEN. **Where's the bear spray?**

HAZEL. **Bear spray?**

AIDEN. **I told you to bring it. Where is it?**

HAZEL. **I forgot it.**

PART ONE: THE ENCOUNTER

AIDEN. **You *forgot* it?**

HAZEL. **You distracted me – I was getting ready, and you –**

She comes closer. Weight shifting, muscle rippling, and at her feet…

Two cubs. Rolling round in the dirt.

OSKAR. Just as Pappa and I run out of things to say, his nurse Karolin appears at the door.

KAROLIN. **Oskar, a word?**

OSKAR. I smile at Pappa, leave him a packet of Smash – chocolate corn snacks, his favourite – and follow Karolin to the hallway. It smells like soup and disinfectant.

HAZEL. She will have smelled the campsite from five miles away.

I'm not like *Christian*-Christian, but I start praying.

Please God, let us be okay. We must be okay. We will be okay, just as long as we –

AIDEN. **RUN!**

HAZEL. Aiden makes a break for it – but the bear is too fast.

Suddenly she is all mouth. Her teeth close around his leg and –

CRUNCH!

OSKAR. I can hear Pappa eating Smash from out here.

Karolin shuts the door.

RIO. Vinnie's shouting at me to come to the break room – but it's like he's on mute.

Four policemen try to corner the stag by the bakery, and I think of Lacey and her cinnamon swirls.

They shoot…

A loud BANG!

And they miss!

I hear the stag yelling again but then realise it's me. This horrible sound is coming from *me* and suddenly I'm –

POLICE. **Miss? What are you doing?**

RIO. I'm running – straight for the loading doors round the back of the fish counter.

The bizzies are distracted, the stag breaks loose and now it's chasing *me*. I hit the door release and the iron shutters roll up way too slowly.

OSKAR. Karolin is wearing her bad-news face.

How's he doing?

KAROLIN. **Better than most.**

OSKAR. We both know he's getting worse.

KAROLIN. **He keeps calling me Sonja.**

OSKAR. **He thinks you're Mamma?**

KAROLIN. **Only sometimes. He must miss her.**

OSKAR. **We all miss her.**

HAZEL. It happens so fast.

RIO. Could this thing *be* any slower?

OSKAR. Karolin takes her time.

KAROLIN. **Oskar, your payment is overdue.**

OSKAR. **I know, Karolin, I'm sorry.**

KAROLIN. **Two months' fees.**

OSKAR. **My business is – held up. I need more time.**

KAROLIN. **We have a long waiting list. Physically, your father is very well – he could live for many years.**

OSKAR. **Let's hope not, eh?**

She doesn't laugh. Because it isn't funny.

KAROLIN. **If he does, we need to know you can afford the payments. I can give you a week.**

OSKAR. I try not to think about the six tours I missed today.

Perfect. I'll have the money – jeg lover.

HAZEL. He is everywhere.

There are… chunks of him. Everywhere.

I hide in a ditch as she throws him round like a rag doll.

I hear the heavy wet sigh of breath. The cracking of bone. There is so much blood.

But he doesn't scream at all.

I think that must be the shock of it.

RIO. Come on, come on, *come on*.

The stag lurches forward –

COME ON – FASTER!

It hurdles the fish counter; I dive out the way; it ducks under the door and then –

Shit. It's stuck.

With one antler jammed under the shutter, it twists its neck –

Wait – you'll hurt yourself!

Something in my voice makes it stop.

And there's a split second where we look at each other. Time becomes liquid. The whole of Tesco melts away and all I can see… is my reflection in the dark pools of its eyes.

And maybe this sounds *mad*, but I swear it's trying to…

CRACK!

With one sharp jerk of its head, the stag breaks free.

…Then disappears, galloping into the night.

HAZEL. When she's done, she slopes off with her cubs.

RIO. I think I'm in shock.

OSKAR. I feel sick.

HAZEL. I feel for my phone. No signal. *Fuck*.

RIO. Vinnie and Martin come out the break room and the bizzies get to asking them questions. But how do you explain that?

OSKAR. Two months' fees in one week and a walrus on my boat.

RIO. Like where did it come from? Did that just happen? Was there *really* a white stag in the Halewood Tesco?

HAZEL. I move to leave, and stumble over…

RIO. I step back and my foot touches…

HAZEL. I look down and my stomach lurches.

RIO. An antler. Must've snapped off on the door… I pick it up.

HAZEL. A bloodied, bright, NASCAR-yellow sneaker.

RIO. It's kinda gross… But also kinda beautiful.

HAZEL. The foot is still inside.

OSKAR. Some things are just impossible.

HAZEL. That's when I throw up.

RIO. Expect a visit from an unusual stranger?

Pause.

Fuck me.

A rumble. Maybe the room shakes a little? Maybe it's a bit melted, a little fuzzy round the edges? Maybe something is growing? Sprouting up through the cracks?

PART TWO: THE EXCHANGE

Time moves forward. OSKAR, RIO *and* HAZEL *are propelled, spun, or otherwise dragged along with it.*

OSKAR. Three days pass and the walrus does not move.

He does not care about two months' fees. Or insurance, food, rent, bills –

The walrus has no idea what he is doing to me. I begin to hate him.

I go to the ticket office to cancel another day's work.

A coach pulls up and vomits out tourists. They bumble around in bright-pink ponchos, cameras going *snap-snap-snap!*

Another coach arrives…

And another…

Until there is a *sea* of ponchos, bobbing round like jellyfish.

I fight my way to the desk.

Hallo, Ingrid.

INGRID. **Another day to cancel, Oskar?**

OSKAR. **Afraid so.**

INGRID. **I'll get it sorted.**

OSKAR. **Takk.**

INGRID. **How is your pappa?**

OSKAR. **He's doing well.**

INGRID. **He was always a very strong man.**

OSKAR. **Ja. Very strong.**

INGRID. **But not always kind.**

Beat.

He's lucky to have you, Oskar.

OSKAR. I do not want to talk about Pappa.

I want to talk about Ingrid.

I want to talk about her morning. Her favourite things. Her least favourite things.

I want to ask –

Is something happening today?

INGRID. **What do you mean?**

OSKAR. **All these people. Is there a flea market?**

INGRID. **Å, nei. They're here for Gjest.**

OSKAR. **Gjest?**

INGRID. **The walrus? He's been all over the news.**

OSKAR. **They gave him a *name*?**

INGRID. **The tourists love him. They're coming from all over.**

OSKAR. **Idioter.**

INGRID. **You sound like your pappa.**

OSKAR. **They cause trouble.**

INGRID. **They spend money, Oskar. The gift shop has never done so well.**

Beat.

A penny drops…

OSKAR. **Of course…**

INGRID. **Of course, what?**

OSKAR. Ingrid is a genius.

PART TWO: THE EXCHANGE 21

INGRID. **Oskar? There's a queue. I must get back to work.**

OSKAR. **Me too, Ingrid. Me too.**

HAZEL. The attack happened early morning. By late evening Aiden's mom has made the flight down from Montana and moved into the apartment.

Nancy is a tiger mom. Her husband Ron died in a palladium mine leaving her with two sons and enough compensation for early retirement.

She makes chamomile tea and lends me all these grief books. As if this is my first time.

I read about the feelings I can expect to feel. I read about denial –

OSKAR. It's quite simple really.

HAZEL. Anger.

OSKAR. The walrus has ruined my life.

HAZEL. Bargaining.

OSKAR. And maybe Pappa is right, maybe it's my fault for becoming a tour guide.

HAZEL. Depression.

OSKAR. Maybe there is no way out.

HAZEL. And acceptance.

OSKAR. Or maybe, there is an opportunity.

Beat.

The tourists spend money for the walrus.

HAZEL. I read about how everything is normal because nothing is normal.

OSKAR (*slower*). The tourists *spend money* for the walrus!

HAZEL. Nancy cancels Aiden's Amex. She rings his boss. She makes butterscotch cookies.

NANCY. **If it's too much, Hazel, we can take care of the funeral – flower arrangements, music choices…**

HAZEL. **It's okay. I need the distraction.**

Zach arrives a few days later. He comes in like a tornado, all wind and fury.

ZACH. **Fucking bear attacks.**

NANCY. **Zachary, Hazel is mourning.**

ZACH. **We're all mourning, mom.**

HAZEL. Zach and Aiden are twins. *Were* twins. Non-identical. Aiden was into computers and British music. Zach is into football and the second amendment.

ZACH. **It's fucking criminal. They let those things run wild.**

HAZEL. The CPW puts out a catch-and-kill order. They want to find and euthanise the bear themselves. But the local hunting community decides to… help out.

When I go to the store, there are men in camo making promises.

HUNTER. **Don't worry, darlin', we're gonna find that animal.**

HAZEL. I can't even go to Starbucks without –

BARISTA. **Sorry about your boyfriend. Do you wanna come on my podcast?**

HAZEL. So I stay inside.

RIO. I get to Lacey's in the afternoon, expecting her to be fuming but when she opens the door, she's like –

LACEY. **Oh my god, is it true?**

RIO. She's a little older than me. From London originally, in her third year at John Moores studying Events Management. She's dead good at it. One day, Lacey wants to run a radical queer feminist music festival.

Is what true?

PART TWO: THE EXCHANGE

LACEY. **The videos are all over Insta. When I saw it, I thought, hey – that's Rio's Tesco! Then I read the caption, and I was like – a stag? Like a stag do? But *then* I was like –**

RIO. She shows me her Instagram.

LACEY. **An actual fucking deer! I mean, what the fuck?**

RIO. It's weird, seeing it there. Like iPhone footage from a dream.

LACEY. **People are losing their minds. They're saying it's some sort of 'sign'. Like it 'means' something.**

RIO. When I close my eyes, I can see the stag. Glowing white and looking right at me –

LACEY. **If it's a sign of anything, it's that you lot need to take the bins out. People are so stupid.**

Beat.

Right, Rio?

RIO. **What?**

LACEY. **People are idiots.**

RIO. **Yeah, no, idiots...**

LACEY. **Anyway, you're famous. I've been showing everyone – the whole of Sapphic Film Soc. They want to meet you, actually, I said you'd come.**

RIO. **Mm?**

LACEY. **It's not just for students. And it's not like – super academic. Townies are welcome, as long as they're lesbians.**

RIO. Lacey's always been like – really sure of her sexuality. At nine years old she was making her Barbies scissor in the playground, by thirteen she'd sworn off boys for life.

When we met, I wasn't really out. I wasn't really *in* either, I just... I wasn't really anything.

LACEY. **Are you okay? You seem spaced.**

RIO. **I'm – yeah. I just feel bad for not texting. For flaking out.**

She kisses me.

I love kissing Lacey. It's boss. It's like… breathtaking.

LACEY. **You're forgiven. Just this once.**

RIO. **I'll make it up to you. I swear.**

LACEY. **Oh yeah? And how are you gonna do that?**

RIO. She pulls me closer, runs a hand through my hair.

LACEY. **You're so soft, baby.**

RIO. And normally that's nice, but for some reason tonight it feels –

LACEY. **I have the fittest girlfriend in the whole of the Liverpool City Region.**

RIO. Like she is *so* gentle, but something just feels –

LACEY. **My girlfriend has the best tits in the whole of the Liverpool City Region.**

RIO. Like, *wrong*, like – *not good* and I can't –

LACEY. **Is that a fucking antler?**

RIO. **I wasn't going to show her, but it's sticking out my bag.**

LACEY. **It's got blood on it, Ree, it's gross.**

RIO. **I couldn't leave it there…**

LACEY. **So you've been carrying it around? It's got diseases or something.**

RIO. **You're right. I'll get rid of it.**

LACEY. **Rio, what are you –**

RIO. **I'll see you later!**

LACEY. **Rio!**

OSKAR. Gjest is quite the celebrity.

> His fan club keeps growing. He teases them; Pappa's boat is behind another, barely visible through the fence.

REPORTER. **Gjest the walrus is enjoying his holiday here in Oslo, but experts have warned the public to give the creature space. The walrus has a right to roam and will eventually return to the water.**

OSKAR. I take Pia to the edge of the crowd and find a jellyfish arguing with a policeman.

TOURIST. **C'mon. Just a bit closer? You come to Norway to see the wildlife and they won't let you *see* the wildlife!**

OSKAR. **What's going on?**

TOURIST. **They won't let us through. Boat owners only. Bullshit.**

Beat.

OSKAR *readies himself. Here goes…*

OSKAR. **I have a boat.**

TOURIST. **You do?**

OSKAR. **I could take you down there. Get some nice close-up shots.**

TOURIST. **Oh dude, you'd do that?**

OSKAR. **Sure. It would be a risk for me, though.**

TOURIST. **I bet. The pigs in this country, huh?**

OSKAR. Jellyfish do not have brains.

Ja. And this boat is my livelihood.

Pause.

TOURIST. **Ohh… I mean, I'd be willing to pay. Say… a thousand kroner?**

OSKAR. **Double it.**

TOURIST. **No way, dude.**

OSKAR. **Suit yourself. Kom, Pia.**

I give him ten seconds. Ni... Åtte... Sju...

TOURIST. **Wait... Half now, half when I have pictures.**

OSKAR. **Come with me. Take that off.**

He removes his poncho, and we head to the gate.

Another policeman appears.

He looks at me. Pia. The tourist. Me again.

I show him my ID. If anything, it's too easy.

HAZEL. The dress Nancy picks out for me is simple but tasteful. Black polyester, so I can't touch anyone without giving them a static shock.

We trail into church like ants behind a coffin she also chose, carried by Zach and five guys from Aiden's software-development firm.

Nancy squeezes my hand. She keeps saying –

NANCY. **Oh.**

HAZEL. Every few minutes, just –

NANCY. **Oh.**

HAZEL. The priest welcomes everyone, then Zach makes a speech. Tells some story from when they were kids, which ends up being more about him than Aiden –

ZACH. **I'm gonna miss you, bro.**

HAZEL. And then it's my turn.

I look out at all these people...

Aiden's friends. Aiden's colleagues. *Aiden's* family.

I invited some people from college, but I guess it's a weekday.

I leave my body.

I float six feet above the podium and watch myself say –

I met Aiden when I was eighteen. We were together for ten years.

He was there for me when my mom died, and I never really knew my dad, so... When he got the job out here, I guess it made sense for me to...

Every day he was the first thing on my mind.

There is a sound coming from outside the church. A rhythmic sort of sound. Quiet at first, perhaps we don't notice it...

He was smart. And ambitious. Although sometimes he could be...

He had a whole future planned out for us – a house, two to three kids, a dog. And now he's gone –

The sound gets louder.

Sorry, uh... Now he's gone...

The sound gets even louder.

Zach is the first to stand.

ZACH. **What the fuck is that noise?**

HAZEL. Nancy tells him to sit.

ZACH. **You don't hear that?**

HAZEL. **Uh... Kids, a dog, and now he's gone, I...**

The sound gets louder.

ZACH. **You're fucking kidding me.**

HAZEL. Zach climbs out the pew and marches down the aisle.

He opens the door, and the noise is –

OSKAR. **Shh! Quiet.**

I lead the tourist down to Pappa's boat.

Æsj! The *smell* – rotting fish and walrus breath. Pia is in heaven.

Gjest barely looks up. Freeloader. Parasitt.

TOURIST. **Whoa. The size of this guy!**

OSKAR. The tourist takes his photos.

> **That's enough.**

TOURIST. **Just a few more…**

OSKAR. **Enough. Someone will see.**

> I take him back up to the gate and down the promenade. He shows me his camera.

TOURIST. *National Geographic*, **eat your heart out.**

OSKAR. **Hvor er pengene mine?**

TOURIST. **I'm sorry?**

OSKAR. **My money?**

TOURIST. **Oh, right. Here.**

OSKAR. **Take my number. If anyone wants to get close to the beast, tell them to call me.**

TOURIST. **Y'know… You're kind of intense.**

HAZEL. Everyone follows Zach out to the cemetery.

> And it is a *blur*.
>
> Someone is beating a drum, the cops are here, a TV crew, there's a crowd across the street, chanting, holding signs:

PLACARD 1. No such thing as a 'problem' bear!

PLACARD 2. Stop the killing!

PLACARD 3. Bears will be bears!

HAZEL. Us, a sullen mass of black.

> Them, a whirling riot of colour.
>
> Each crowd its own animal, staring the other down.

ZACH. **This is my brother's funeral, you hippy fucks!**

PLACARD 1. I feel a hand on my elbow, look up to see Nancy.

NANCY. **Come on, Hazel. Let's get out of here.**

HAZEL. **What do they want?**

NANCY. **Animal-rights nuts. They're mad about the kill order.**

HAZEL. And that's when I catch her eye.

> A redhead. I know she sees me too because she nods.
>
> And I can just tell, like somehow, I just *know*, she has never believed in anything so much as she believes in this.
>
> She holds her sign up high:
>
> YOU CAN'T PUNISH INSTINCT.
>
> Zach grabs a stone from the path, weighs it in his hand, then lets it fly.

ZACH. **Fucking animals! Whose side are you on?**

HAZEL. It hits the redhead just above the eye. She doesn't even flinch.

RIO. I leave Lacey's, get back to Mum's and am halfway through the door when –

MICK. **Rio, kidda, hang fire –**

RIO. **Oh, hiya, Mick.**

> Cosmic Mick is Mum's next-door neighbour.

MICK. **How's your Lacey?**

RIO. **She's… Yeah. Things feel a bit off with us – with me. I can't work it out.**

> Back in the day, Mick ran a head shop in Quiggins – this is when Quiggins *was* Quiggins – now he just spends a lot of time on the internet.
>
> Which means sometimes he has wonky ideas about 5G and vaccinations, but mostly it means he says stuff like –

MICK. **Not surprised. Strange vibes in the cosmos.**

Beat.

I heard about your white hart.

RIO. **My what?**

MICK. **The stag, kidda, the stag!**

RIO. **Oh. People are saying it's a sign...**

MICK. **Well, you saw it up close. What d'you reckon?**

RIO. **I dunno.**

MICK. **I think you might. Else why are you carrying round that antler?**

RIO. **It sounds mad.**

MICK. **Not to me.**

Pause.

RIO. **There was a moment... where it looked at me. The stag. We looked at each other. And I had this feeling like... Like it was gonna show me something.**

Mick produces a vape, smokes it like a philosopher.

MICK. **I've been reading about King Arthur. On the Wikipedia? You see, Rio, in Arthurian legend, the white hart is a symbol of man's spiritual quest. He who hunts the stag will have some great truth revealed to him.**

RIO. **What are you saying, Mick?**

MICK. **I'm saying a white stag in the Halewood Tesco has got to *mean* something. Perhaps Liverpool has been chosen.**

RIO. **For what?**

MICK. **Beats me. But there's only one way to find out... We go after it.**

RIO. **We?**

MICK. **You and me, kidda!**

RIO. **I dunno, Mick –**

MICK. **Seven p.m. tomorrow. Bring the antler.**

PART TWO: THE EXCHANGE   31

RIO. Then he vanishes in a cloud of Triple Mango.

HAZEL. The cops break up the protest, and everyone moves on. Zach and his uncles have planned a bear hunt in lieu of a wake.

   I hang back and find the redhead behind the church. It's like she's waiting for me.

SAM. **It's not personal. The picket.**

HAZEL. **I mean it's... kinda screwed up.**

SAM. **So's killing a bear. A hundred and twenty euthanised last year. For what?**

   Beat.

   I'm Sam, by the way.

HAZEL. **I'm sorry about my... Zach.**

SAM. **The asshole? Why are *you* sorry?**

   Pause. She doesn't know.

HAZEL. **I liked your sign.**

SAM. **You did?**

HAZEL. **That thing about instinct? Makes sense. Her cubs needed food – she found a campsite, so...**

   Sam leans in. Like we're at summer camp, telling secrets.

SAM. **The cops didn't say she had cubs.**

HAZEL. **Uh – yeah, she – didn't they? I think maybe that's why she attacked us? They looked kinda thin. Someone left a cooler like way outside the campground.**

   I'm just telling her what happened, right? I am *allowed* to tell people...

   But now she's smiling. And I know why.

   She doesn't even have to say it.

   What mother wouldn't protect her babies?

RIO. That night, I dream of the stag. It looks at me, curious, like it belongs in the dream and I'm the one trespassing. Trespassing in my own head...

So even though it feels like a really bad idea, and even though Lacey would *murder* us if she knew, I find myself waiting for Cosmic Mick at the edge of the woods...

He arrives, fifteen minutes late, I shit you not, in a full suit of armour, riding an e-scooter.

And he's not alone.

MICK. **Sorry, kidda. Should've said. I might've told a few friends about our plan and, well... we're not the only ones who think the stag has a message.**

RIO. There are five blokes. It's the full spectrum: North Face, Everton shirt, Armani suit, M&S chinos and –

MICK. **Tony here even has some hunting experience. On Xbox like, but it's something.**

RIO. Tony looks like your best mate's dad. Except harder and when he speaks, everyone listens.

TONY. **So this is the lad with the antler?**

RIO. Lad... This happens sometimes. People think I'm – and it's always really awkward and I never know what to –

MICK. **Show him, Rio.**

RIO. So I do.

Tony claps a hand on my shoulder. It feels like I'm being knighted.

TONY. **Nice one, son. We should call you Braveheart.**

RIO. And just like that, I'm in. These lads are my brothers. And the hunt begins tonight!

OSKAR. News travels fast. The tourist tells another, who tells another... They gossip over their continental breakfasts in their luxury hotels. Soon, I am fully booked.

Roll up, roll up for Gjest the Walrus! The Scandinavian Spectacle! The Nightmare from the North!

I should not say this but… fuck Janteloven, I'm making double what I used to.

I hand over two months' fees – in cash. Karolin tries to hide her surprise.

Relief floods my body like a glass of akevitt.

I walk to Pappa's room and *æsj*… There is a smell.

Shall I open a window, Pappa?

Fresh air drifts in with the song of a blackbird in the cherry tree.

It reminds me of Mamma. Whistling in the kitchen.

How are you feeling?

PAPPA. **How is the boat?**

OSKAR. **The boat is fine.**

The same conversation, every time.

PAPPA. **Mackerel season soon. I want you on double shift.**

OSKAR. **Double shift?**

PAPPA. **I'll pay you extra.**

Beat.

OSKAR. **What's my name?**

PAPPA. **Unnskyld?**

OSKAR. **My name, what is it?**

PAPPA. **Lars, don't be foolish.**

Pause.

OSKAR. **Pappa, Lars moved to Luxembourg. To look after his mother.**

PAPPA. **Er det riktig?**

OSKAR. **Do you know who I am?**

Something shifts. The world tilting, groaning, capsizing…

His face grows hard. Like I am seven years old and telling him I feel seasick.

He wrings his hands. His leather-thick fisherman's hands. Criss-crossed with scars from hooks and filleting knives…

I am a stranger.

And it is as though the whole world has tilted.

And yet at exactly the same time…

Nothing has changed.

RIO. The hunt rides for three nights with no sign of the stag.

I swerve work. I swerve Mum. I even swerve Lacey, because for some reason – this is the only thing that matters.

I don't spend much time with men. Besides Martin – but this lot are totally different. They get emotional. About their kids, their dads, their bodies… Jürgen Klopp.

We talk a lot. Me and the lads. We talk about the city – about hen-do hotels and austerity. About feeling proud and torn all at once.

We talk about girls. I tell them about Lacey and how stunning she is, how lucky I am that she chose me – and how… I just want to be good enough for her.

We talk about how the stag might change things. Cos it feels like things need to change.

And when I'm with them, it's like I've got a suit of armour and all. We bump fists and butt heads, and I feel *invincible*.

I like being Braveheart. I like the person they think I am.

HAZEL. I forget about Sam the activist until a cop car shows up at the apartment.

Zach is first to the door.

PART TWO: THE EXCHANGE 35

ZACH. **Did they get it?**

HAZEL. The officer looks twelve years old. He is visibly sweating.

OFFICER. **The bear *has* been captured –**

ZACH. **And shot. You shot it, right?**

OFFICER. **Please, Mr Erickson, I'm here to speak with Ms Curtis.**

HAZEL. **What's going on?**

OFFICER. **The bear is in captivity, but there has been some information shared with us –**

ZACH. **What fucking information? From who?**

OFFICER. **We've been told the bear was not alone during the attack, is that correct?**

HAZEL. **She had cubs, yeah.**

ZACH. **What does that have to do with anything?**

OFFICER. **It changes the circumstances from a... Well, an unprovoked, random attack to a defensive, protective –**

ZACH. **Don't you fucking say it.**

OFFICER. **Somehow the fact of the cubs has reached the public sphere. And it seems there is a lot of sympathy broadly speaking, for a er – mamma bear, and...**

HAZEL. And public opinion is powerful. Powerful enough to mount a legal challenge to the kill order. There will be a hearing to decide if the bear lives or dies.

ZACH. **A hearing? What's it gonna do, object?**

HAZEL. I am invited to give evidence. They want me to prepare a statement.

The officer leaves.

Beat.

ZACH. **You never mentioned any cubs.**

HAZEL. **I'm sorry… I didn't know it was important.**

ZACH gets really close to HAZEL. Uncomfortably close, invading her space.

ZACH. **You're going to fix this. You're going to tell them what that thing did to my brother. Do you understand?**

Beat.

HAZEL *nods.*

RIO. By night four, things are getting tense.

Tony demands a meeting.

TONY. **This isn't fucking working. Four nights, and we haven't even *seen* it.**

MICK. **We just need to keep looking. It can't have gone far.**

RIO. Tony asks for his bag. North Face has been carrying it like a golf caddy.

He takes out a crossbow.

What's that?

TONY. **D'you like it? Our Steven got it us from America.**

RIO. **What do you need it for?**

Tony smiles, like he always does. Mick says –

MICK. **Rio, kidda, don't stress.**

RIO. **No, what does he need that for?**

TONY. **Are you serious? We're hunting a stag, Braveheart.**

RIO. **But you're not supposed to kill it. Right, Mick? You hunt the stag as in – you try to find it, but you don't *shoot* it.**

TONY. **But we've been hunting, haven't we? I reckon this friggin' magic deer, whatever message it has, is only gonna be revealed if we *take* it. If we win the prize.**

PART TWO: THE EXCHANGE   37

RIO. **It's not about a prize –**

TONY. **No? What about your antler, Braveheart?** *You've* **got a trophy. I'd like one too.**

RIO. The lads are nodding, like this was always the plan.

TONY. **If you're not with us – if you're not one of us – then you should leave.**

RIO. Tony pushes on through the trees, crossbow in the crook of his shoulder.

Mick hesitates. But he doesn't look back.

HAZEL. The time before the hearing passes *slowly*.

Aiden always said impatience was my biggest flaw. Impatience, and people-pleasing.

The apartment has one bed, which Nancy has taken. The bathroom is filled with her creams and HRT tablets. Zach drinks a six-pack every night, then passes out on the couch.

I have a cot in Aiden's home office, but I don't sleep. I just stare at my computer and try to write a statement.

I start doomscrolling for inspiration. Hashtag ColoradoBearTrial.

TWEET 1. **Soooo tragic. Only fair the bear is shot. RIP.**

TWEET 2. **Don't blame it. I'd kill more skinny cishet boys if I could.**

TWEET 3. **They should do a movie about this. Halle Bailey would EAT as the girl.**

HAZEL. I find an article. A picture of this young couple. Really young. It says the greatest tragedy is that they were trying to start a family. And now they never will.

NANCY. **What are you doing?**

HAZEL. She stands at the door, swaying a little.

I can't sleep.

Pause.

Are you okay, Nancy?

She stares, glassy-eyed, at Aiden's Cornell certificate.

NANCY. **It's just so sad. You lost them both.**

Pause.

I'm not saying the miscarriage was your fault… but maybe it was a blessing.

HAZEL. **I don't know what you mean.**

NANCY. **I had two kids when Ron died. Had to raise them alone. I'm not complaining. But I don't think you could, darlin'. I don't think you could've done it. It's not in your nature.**

Beat.

HAZEL. I think if I spend another minute in this apartment I might explode.

It's late, Nancy. Go back to bed.

RIO. The lads disappear and I'm alone in the woods.

The antler feels heavy in my bag.

My phone is pinging with messages from Lacey, Mum, Martin, everyone *fuming*, so I turn it off and chuck it as far away as I can.

Then I sort of regret doing that. Cos I don't know my way back.

HAZEL. The next day, I pay fifteen dollars to enter the animal sanctuary.

You have to go in through the gift shop. Shelves stuffed with cuddly bears.

I follow the signs to a viewing deck looking out over a meadow. There's a board that tells you all the bears' names. Baloo, Winnie, Smokey, Koda…

Aiden's bear isn't on the board. She doesn't have a name.

PART TWO: THE EXCHANGE

RIO. I try to retrace our steps.

OSKAR. I leave the care home and find myself at the pier.

RIO. Total darkness ahead but then…

OSKAR. Show my ID.

RIO. A gap between the branches.

OSKAR. Through the gate.

RIO. A clearing. Everything is blue and purple and silver. Like we're not in Liverpool any more, we're on an alien planet.

HAZEL. I stand there for a half-hour.

I'm ready to give up when… There. No. *There*. She hauls out her den.

OSKAR. And there he is.

RIO. The stag walks in.

OSKAR. The mighty walrus.

RIO. After four nights of searching, the stag walks in like 'Sorry I'm late.'

HAZEL. She's far away, but unmistakable.

OSKAR/RIO/HAZEL. Hello, stranger.

Pause. They are all captivated. The earth moves.

HAZEL. I open my notes app.

OSKAR. It is, for the first time, just the two of us.

HAZEL. **The bear murdered Aiden and for that reason…**

OSKAR. His eyes are tiny –

HAZEL. **The bear killed my…**

OSKAR. His tusks longer than my arm –

HAZEL. **The bear is a wild animal and…**

OSKAR. His back covered in lines and scars…

HAZEL. **The bear...**

Radiates danger.

The bear is buzzing with don't-fuck-with-me-I-swear-to-God energy.

The bear isn't sorry.

The bear has never been sorry, or sweet, or small.

RIO. The stag stands in the clearing.

OSKAR. The walrus reclines.

HAZEL. And then looks at me.

RIO. He looks at me...

OSKAR. Han ser på meg.

HAZEL. Stares me down.

RIO. Sizes me up. And I think this must be it. Like, he's *rewarding* me for leaving the hunt, for drawing a line... This is the moment. He's gonna show me something.

OSKAR. I look right back.

HAZEL. I try to ask her –

RIO. **What is it? What's wrong with me? Why don't I feel right?**

I put the antler down between us – a peace offering.

HAZEL. Try to put myself in her paws...

OSKAR. You're never going to leave, are you?

HAZEL. Would you rather be put to sleep? Or stay locked in here?

RIO. And the stag steps closer.

HAZEL. What sort of choice is that?

RIO. So close, I can see myself in the dark pools of its eyes –

Tall and strong and hard and sharp and really *fucking* majestic and then –

PART TWO: THE EXCHANGE   41

HAZEL. I wish someone would tell me what to do. I wish my mom were here.

OSKAR. I give up.

RIO. It takes a shit.

   I'm stood there, waiting for a sign –

   And the stag lifts its tail and lets out a shower of pellets.

OSKAR. You win, Gjest.

RIO. Then nuzzles the ground, starts chewing. And I can see what it's eating –

OSKAR. **Faen! You win!**

RIO. Fucking Wotsits. Fucking *litter*. And that's when it hits me.

OSKAR. Gjest winks. The walrus *winks* at me.

RIO. It's not a sign. Or a symbol. Or a fucking metaphor.

HAZEL. And I wonder… where are her cubs?

RIO. And I've never felt so… embarrassed.

HAZEL. She had two cubs, where are they?

RIO. Because Lacey was right. It's just a stag.

HAZEL. Maybe she doesn't care. Maybe she's relieved.

OSKAR. This is your boat now. Have it.

HAZEL. I was relieved.

RIO. It's not going to fix anything.

HAZEL. When I saw the blood, I felt relieved. And I know that's not the right feeling to have. And it was years ago, and I'm probably the very worst sort of person but…

OSKAR. I don't want it.

HAZEL. Because it didn't feel right. And if you feel that in your gut, it can't be a wrong feeling, can it? And now it's happening again. It happened *again*. Blood. Relief.

OSKAR. And the walrus doesn't know who I am.

HAZEL. The bear has no idea what's about to happen.

OSKAR. He doesn't care.

HAZEL. But that's just another day, isn't it? For her. That's just another day.

OSKAR. He cares so little he turns his back.

HAZEL. She doesn't walk the path, she *makes* the fucking path.

RIO. The stag is just a stag, and I am just... me.

OSKAR. So why try? Why am I trying?

Pause.

It's time to go home.

The world erupts into chaos. Colours, sounds, smells – everything is up for grabs. OSKAR, RIO *and* HAZEL *are chewed up...*

PART THREE: THE AFTERMATH

And spat out. They take stock of the room, the audience, each other. It all looks a little different. Has stuff been moved? Have the colours changed? Is there grass? A smell? This is the same room, isn't it? Like, I'm pretty au fait with rooms, but this one's a bit… weird.

OSKAR. In the morning, I stop at the bakery on the way to Ingrid's flat.

You can tell which window is hers because of the flowers.

I ring the bell. I know exactly what I am going to say.

Eight years we have worked together and *now* I know what I am going to say.

INGRID. **Oskar? Where have you been? Pia was waiting.**

OSKAR. **Hallo, Ingrid.**

Pia pushes through her legs and licks my fingers.

Did she behave?

INGRID. **As always.**

OSKAR. **I have something for you.**

I hand over the box.

INGRID. **Kanelbolle?**

OSKAR. Still warm, dusted with brown sugar.

For å si takk. For your help. Taking care of Pia… Taking care of me.

Beat.

INGRID. **Has something happened?**

OSKAR. **I want to ask you to come for dinner. With me. Tonight.**

Pause.

INGRID. **Oskar, I can't.**

OSKAR. **Another night maybe?**

She hands back the box.

INGRID. **I know what you've been doing.**

OSKAR. **Unnskyld?**

INGRID. **With Gjest. Everyone is talking about it. I have tourists asking after you.**

OSKAR. **I can explain. I needed money. For Pappa's care –**

INGRID. **Gjest is a wild animal, Oskar, not a tourist attraction. No one was supposed to get close.**

OSKAR. **They would have done it anyway. If it wasn't me, then –**

INGRID. **It *was* you. You encouraged them. And now he's going to pay for it.**

OSKAR. **What?**

INGRID. **This morning. He nearly killed a fisherman. So now they're going to…**

OSKAR. **But no one was hurt?**

INGRID. **It was enough. Apparently, he is too dangerous. He doesn't belong here.**

OSKAR. **Then he shouldn't have come.**

INGRID. **Do you know why the walrus is here, Oskar?**

OSKAR. **Jeg vet ikke. To punish me?**

INGRID. **He's here because of us. And this is the welcome we give him?**

OSKAR. **Ingrid, please –**

She shuts the door. Pia looks at me. Sad brown eyes.

HAZEL. The courtroom is less impressive than I imagined.

I guess I pictured like a *12 Angry Men* kinda set-up, y'know?

But really, it's just… few tables, microphones, glasses of water.

Nancy offered to help pick my outfit.

NANCY. **You don't want to look like you're enjoying the attention.**

HAZEL. I have never enjoyed attention.

I choose a green pantsuit I bought years ago for a job interview. The tags are still on.

The hearing begins with a land acknowledgement.

JUDGE. **We meet today on the ancestral lands of the Ute people, the original peoples of Colorado who were forcibly removed from this place. We would like to thank them for their ongoing stewardship and hospitality.**

HAZEL. Zach rolls his eyes. The judge calls people up one by one. Wildlife experts, park rangers…

WILDLIFE EXPERT. **As bear habitats are further encroached upon by human activity, interspecies encounters will become more frequent. But currently, *any* kind of attack is extremely rare, and we can't let the actions of one animal colour our perception of an entire species –**

HAZEL. Zach's eye-roll becomes a groan. On to the next guy…

LOCAL COUNCILLOR. **This is not a culling order for an entire species, this is a proportionate response to a tragic event in which a young man was brutally killed. Let's not lose sight of what's important: the grief of a family who deserve peace of mind.**

HAZEL. And then it's my turn. I have my statement in a plastic wallet.

I know exactly what I'm going to say.

Pause. HAZEL *makes her way to the microphone. She takes a moment.*

Nobody deserves to die the way Aiden did.

But before I tell you the details, I just want to say…

HAZEL *surveys the room. She has everyone's complete and undivided attention.*

I do not believe the bear should be euthanised. Nor should it be held in captivity.

It's a wild animal. Attacker or protector, cubs or not, it is alive.

You can't punish instinct.

RIO. I run out of the woods and don't stop until I get to Lacey's.

It's properly dark now. The moon's hanging over her chimney.

I don't know what I'm going to say. I just need to see her.

But the second she opens the door, all beautiful and livid and smelling of Lush… I find I can't speak at all.

LACEY. **What are *you* doing here?**

RIO. **Lacey, I…**

LACEY. **You know what, I don't even want to know.**

RIO. **Please! I need to talk to you.**

LACEY. *Now* **you want to talk? After ghosting me for a week? You didn't show up at work, I even tried your Mum, she was in hysterics. Rio, I was *worried*.**

RIO. **I know, but – I want to explain.**

HAZEL. I tell them the whole story. Every gory detail.

When I finish there's this stunned silence. Like, *surely*, she made that up?

I mean, the foot in the sneaker? That *has* to be made up.

The judge goes into her little decision-making room.

And leaves us to wait.

OSKAR. I take Pia down to the water.

As soon as I arrive, the jellyfish descend.

TOURIST. **There he is! Walrus guy!**

OSKAR. Beyond the fence two policemen are heading for Pappa's boat.

TOURIST. **Hey, look! They're gonna shoot it!**

OSKAR. I head for the gate, present my ID.

POLICE. **Not today.**

OSKAR. **But that's my boat.**

POLICE. **I'm sorry. Det er forbudt.**

OSKAR. The jellyfish crowd around me.

Ingrid hates me.

Pappa is gone.

I have no boat.

No job.

No friends.

I have... nothing to lose.

Pia pulls at her lead, straining for the water.

She looks at me as if to say... *Kom, Oskar.*

I'm still holding the kanelbolle.

(*Giving them to a tourist.*) **For you. Komplimenter fra Oslo.**

    I grip Pia's lead.

    And we run.

HAZEL. The judge reappears after what feels like hours.

    She sits at her microphone and takes a sip of water.

    There's a heavy pause…

JUDGE. **My verdict is as follows. On the basis of today's evidence, I have decided…**

HAZEL. What is this? *American Idol*?

JUDGE. **…to grant the bear – subject PT40 – a reprieve. The euthanasia order will be overturned, and the animal will be taken to a secure facility in Idaho, where it will live the remainder of its life in captivity. That's all, thank you.**

    Pause.

    I can feel Zach's eyes boring into the back of my neck.

RIO. Lacey is proper glaring –

LACEY. **Where the fuck have you been? Why are you covered in mud?**

RIO. **I've been with Cosmic Mick. We were hunting the stag.**

    For the first time in her life, she's speechless.

LACEY. **You've been avoiding me because you've been hunting a white stag with lunatic conspiracy theorists?**

RIO. **I know how it sounds –**

LACEY. **It sounds like bullshit, Rio.**

RIO. **But you were right. It's not a sign. It's not an omen.**

LACEY. **And you had to hang out with crusty Flat Earthers to realise that?**

RIO. **Yeah, well, no – it's not like that – they're nice lads. And actually, I think it's a bit rich for you to make fun of**

people for believing in stuff when *you* blame everything on being an Aries rising.

Wrong thing to say.

I just – I wanted to say sorry for disappearing, but it's over now, so yeah. That's it.

LACEY. **No, Rio, that's not 'it'. What's going on?**

RIO. **Nothing. Honest. I don't know.**

LACEY. **You've been acting weird for weeks. Slow down and talk to me.**

Pause. RIO *tries to find the words.*

RIO. **I just – I... I wanted it to be a sign. I *really* wanted it to be.**

LACEY. **Why?**

RIO. **Because something doesn't feel right. *I* don't feel right. In my skin. I feel like I'm – like I've been wearing my T-shirt inside out, and the label's sticking out and I'm the last to know.**

I'm not making sense. But I've started now.

And when I was with the lads – I didn't feel like that. Being with them made me feel good –

LACEY. **And being with me doesn't?**

RIO. **No – that's – I love you, Lacey.**

LACEY. **Then I don't understand.**

RIO. **The stag is just a stag. It is completely itself. And everyone is always telling me who I am, what I am... But none of it fits.**

LACEY. **Okay...**

RIO. **And the lads think I'm... And that made me feel closer to *me* than I've ever... And sometimes when I'm with you, you make me feel like – like the girl, and I know that's not – politically – but it's not about –**

LACEY. **Rio, breathe –**

RIO. **I don't think I am the girl. And I'm not saying I think I'm a boy, but... I don't know what I am.**

Beat.

You're so sure of yourself, Lacey. And I love that about you. But if I change, if something about me is – is different, then that changes us. And I'm scared that you won't... Like would I still be welcome at Sapphic Film Soc? And – and I don't want to lose you. But I understand. If you don't want... me. I'd get it.

Pause.

LACEY. **I'm sorry, Rio.**

RIO. **It's okay.**

LACEY. **No, let me –**

RIO. **You don't need to explain, honest. I'll leave you to it.**

LACEY. **Fucksake, Ree! I'm sorry I didn't see you.**

Beat.

I mean, I wish you'd just – said something, but... Maybe I don't make that easy.

RIO. Lacey smiles.

LACEY. **Of course, I want you. Even if you're not sure, even if you don't know, even if you *never* know... You're amazing. I love you. I'm not going anywhere.**

RIO. And her smile is like a switch that lights me up. Blackpool Illuminations.

LACEY. **You're so handsome, you know that?**

RIO. And that word feels... She pulls me close. And the hug doesn't make me feel small. It makes me feel *big*. Tall and strong and something close to myself and –

LACEY. **What the fuck?**

RIO. I follow her gaze, right over my shoulder.

I don't believe what I'm seeing.

OSKAR. Pia and I push through the gate and over to Pappa's boat.

The walrus throws his weight around.

The tourists take picture after picture.

Armed policemen inch closer.

POLICE. **Clear the area, this animal is dangerous!**

OSKAR. I stand in front of the boat.

You all need to leave.

Pia bares her teeth.

This is my boat, and you all need to leave.

RIO. The stag is trotting down Lacey's road.

Casual as anything, lopsided with its one antler. Looks smaller out here than it did in Tesco.

Her neighbours come out and stare in disbelief.

No one knows what to do.

And it's not a sign. It doesn't *mean* anything. It's not *for* us.

But it is sort of... magic.

OSKAR. And then it happens.

RIO. A Citroën C3 comes round the corner and the stag isn't quick enough.

OSKAR. It happens so fast I can barely –

RIO. The bonnet creases. The windscreen shatters.

OSKAR. The policeman fires his gun.

RIO. The car swerves onto the pavement, dragging the stag, mangled, and broken, bright-red blood on snow-white fur.

OSKAR. Gjest lurches forward, unharmed but angry.

His tusks slice the air and –

Pia!

She howls – then whimpers…

RIO. It splutters, neck twisted, eyes rolling –

OSKAR. I see her look for me.

Her hind legs go limp.

Pia…

The crowd falls silent.

RIO. Everyone gathers round the body.

OSKAR. And they watch…

RIO. Like kids, waiting for a piñata to split. I pull the remaining antler from the wreckage –

OSKAR. As Gjest pulls his tusk from her body like an almighty sword.

RIO. And I see it –

OSKAR. He rolls off Pappa's sinking piece of junk.

RIO. I see the moment –

OSKAR. He swims away.

RIO. A flicker passes across every face…

Something else is alive. Something else is real.

HAZEL. Everyone files out of the courtroom.

There are reporters and protestors waiting outside.

I look for Sam but can't find her.

My chest feels full. I feel… hormonal. Y'know? Like I might cry.

Nancy comes over, clutching her purse.

I wait for her to yell. Slap me. Spit in my face.

But she doesn't.

She just looks at me. *Really* looks, like she's seeing me for the first time.

And just as she opens her mouth –

ZACH. **You bitch.**

HAZEL. Zach storms over.

ZACH. **You fucking bitch. What the fuck was that?**

NANCY. **She did her best.**

ZACH. **She supported the fucking bear, Mom.**

HAZEL. **I did what I thought was right.**

ZACH. **You're sick. You've always been sick. I knew it, and I told Aiden, years ago I said – if she can't keep a fucking baby in her fucking stomach –**

NANCY. **Zachary, I'm warning you.**

ZACH. **That thing killed my brother, that thing killed your boyfriend –**

HAZEL. **It's not a thing.**

ZACH. **It deserves to be shot. It deserves to be strung up. And you –**

HAZEL. He grabs my arm.

His meaty high-school quarterback fingers close around my arm.

The whole world melts away and I –

ZACH. **FUCK.**

HAZEL. He lets go.

ZACH. **You fucking bit me?**

HAZEL. I can taste his blood. Like hot metal.

ZACH. **You're psychotic. Mom? Do something, Mom. Fuck!**

HAZEL. Nancy doesn't say a word.

> She puts a hand on my cheek. Then looks at her son.
>
> Then turns around…
>
> And just like that…

OSKAR. Time passes.

RIO. Few months, maybe.

OSKAR. Few weeks.

HAZEL. A year.

RIO. Time feels a bit weird after that.

OSKAR. Ingrid and I bury Pia.

> I tell her I'm sorry.
>
> For Gjest. For everything.
>
> We agree to begin again.
>
> She helps me apply for a loan to repair the boat.
>
> In the time it takes to fix it, I persuade Karolin of my idea.
>
> There's a lot of paperwork, but eventually she agrees.
>
> I help Pappa onto the deck.
>
> We head out into the fjord.
>
> On your right, you will see the Norwegian National Opera and Ballet House.
>
> Up ahead, Hovedøya Island, the ruins of a Cistercian monastery…
>
> Pappa doesn't care about any of that.
>
> His map of these waters is tattered and damp, but fragments rise to the surface.

PAPPA. **You used to find more sea trout in the central fjord. But now all these tourists – their cruises and jet skis…**

OSKAR. I switch the engine off and we drift.

You're not too cold?

PAPPA. **Worry about yourself.**

Pause.

OSKAR. **I need to tell you something.**

PAPPA *does not react. Does he hear* OSKAR*?*

We lost sight of each other after Mamma died. I know you find change difficult. I wish we'd talked. You were unkind.

Beat.

Jeg elsker deg. Jeg tilgir deg.

A long pause. PAPPA *looks at* OSKAR.

PAPPA. **Du ligner så mye på moren din.**

OSKAR. **I do?**

PAPPA. **You have her eyes.**

OSKAR. His lips twitch under his whiskers.

Then he puts a hand on mine.

And his skin is rough leather, criss-crossed with scars.

As he leans, the shift in weight tilts the boat.

Without thinking, I lean back to counterbalance.

An instinct.

Something in our nature, maybe.

RIO. Night falls and I go to the woods.

HAZEL. Day breaks, and I head for the canyon.

RIO. It rained yesterday, the smell is still fresh.

HAZEL. I woke up in my apartment to the smell of wet paint.

I'm redecorating.

It's early, not warm yet, but it will be.

I stretch out – muscles tensing, relaxing...

And then I run.

RIO. I reach the clearing.

I can't stay long. Me and Lacey are going dancing later. Sonic Yootha.

I find the antlers right where I left them.

OSKAR. And we sit there, me and Pappa.

The boat bobbing along.

Sky reflected in the water.

RIO. They weren't mine to keep.

And the woods have taken them back.

HAZEL. Four miles of the Red Rock Canyon trail.

In the shadow of Pikes Peak, reaching for the stars.

And on the trail ahead of me – two cubs, hiding in the brush.

RIO. Neon-green moss spread over bone; grooves gnawed by squirrels.

The prongs a scaffold for fat spiders, pearls of dew.

HAZEL. I keep my distance, wish them luck – watch them disappear into a future that isn't ready for them.

RIO. The stag is remade, over and over, completely itself and everything else.

HAZEL. Then I turn around and head the other way.

RIO. I breathe in the night and shed my skin.

OSKAR. I watch the sun sink into the water.

HAZEL. I run and I run.

RIO. Let go of everything that was given to me, that I never asked for –

HAZEL. Till I'm breathless.

OSKAR. Until the sky burns orange, purple, and pink.

HAZEL. And I don't know why it took me so long –

RIO. I can't believe I never saw it before –

OSKAR. I am more certain now than I have ever been that –

OSKAR/RIO/HAZEL. This is the most beautiful place on Earth.

OSKAR. We look at the same scene with different eyes.

Sitting in our own little worlds.

Separate, but touching.

The End.

A Nick Hern Book

The Walrus Has a Right to Adventure first published in Great Britain as a paperback original in 2022 by Nick Hern Books Limited, The Glasshouse, 49a Goldhawk Road, London W12 8QP in association with Liverpool Everyman & Playhouse Theatres.

The Walrus Has a Right to Adventure copyright © 2025 Billie Collins

Billie Collins has asserted their right to be identified as the author of this work

Cover image: Kerry Spicer

Designed and typeset by Nick Hern Books, London
Printed in Great Britain by Mimeo Ltd, Huntingdon, Cambridgeshire PE29 6XX

A CIP catalogue record for this book is available from the British Library

ISBN 978 1 83904 492 2

CAUTION All rights whatsoever in this play are strictly reserved. Requests to reproduce the text in whole or in part should be addressed to the publisher. This book may not be used, in whole or in part, for the development or training of artificial intelligence technologies or systems.

Amateur Performing Rights Applications for performance, including readings and excerpts, by amateurs in the English language should be addressed to the Performing Rights Manager, Nick Hern Books, The Glasshouse, 49a Goldhawk Road, London W12 8QP, *tel* +44 (0)20 8749 4953, *email* rights@nickhernbooks.co.uk, except as follows:

Australia: ORiGiN Theatrical, *tel* +61 (2) 8514 5201, *email* enquiries@originmusic.com.au, *web* www.origintheatrical.com.au

New Zealand: Play Bureau, 20 Rua Street, Mangapapa, Gisborne 4010, *tel* +64 21 258 3998, *email* info@playbureau.com

United States of America and Canada: The Agency (London) Ltd, see details below

Professional Performing Rights Applications for performance by professionals in any medium and in any language throughout the world (and amateur and stock performances in the United States of America and Canada) should be addressed to The Agency (London) Ltd, 24 Pottery Lane, Holland Park, London W11 4LZ, *fax* +44 (0)20 7727 9037, *email* info@theagency.co.uk

No performance of any kind may be given unless a licence has been obtained. Applications should be made before rehearsals begin. Publication of this play does not necessarily indicate its availability for amateur performance.

www.nickhernbooks.co.uk/environmental-policy

Nick Hern Books' authorised representative in the EU is
Easy Access System Europe – Mustamäe tee 50, 10621 Tallinn, Estonia
email gpsr.requests@easproject.com

www.nickhernbooks.co.uk

@nickhernbooks